Czech
• PICTURE BOOK •

Czech Pictorial Dictionary
(Color and Learn)

WAI CHEUNG

Contents

1. Family 01
2. Body Parts 05
3. Food 09
4. Around the House 13
5. Kitchen 17
6. Bathroom - Dinning room 21
7. Clothes 25
8. Animals 29

Family
Rodina

Body Parts
Části těla

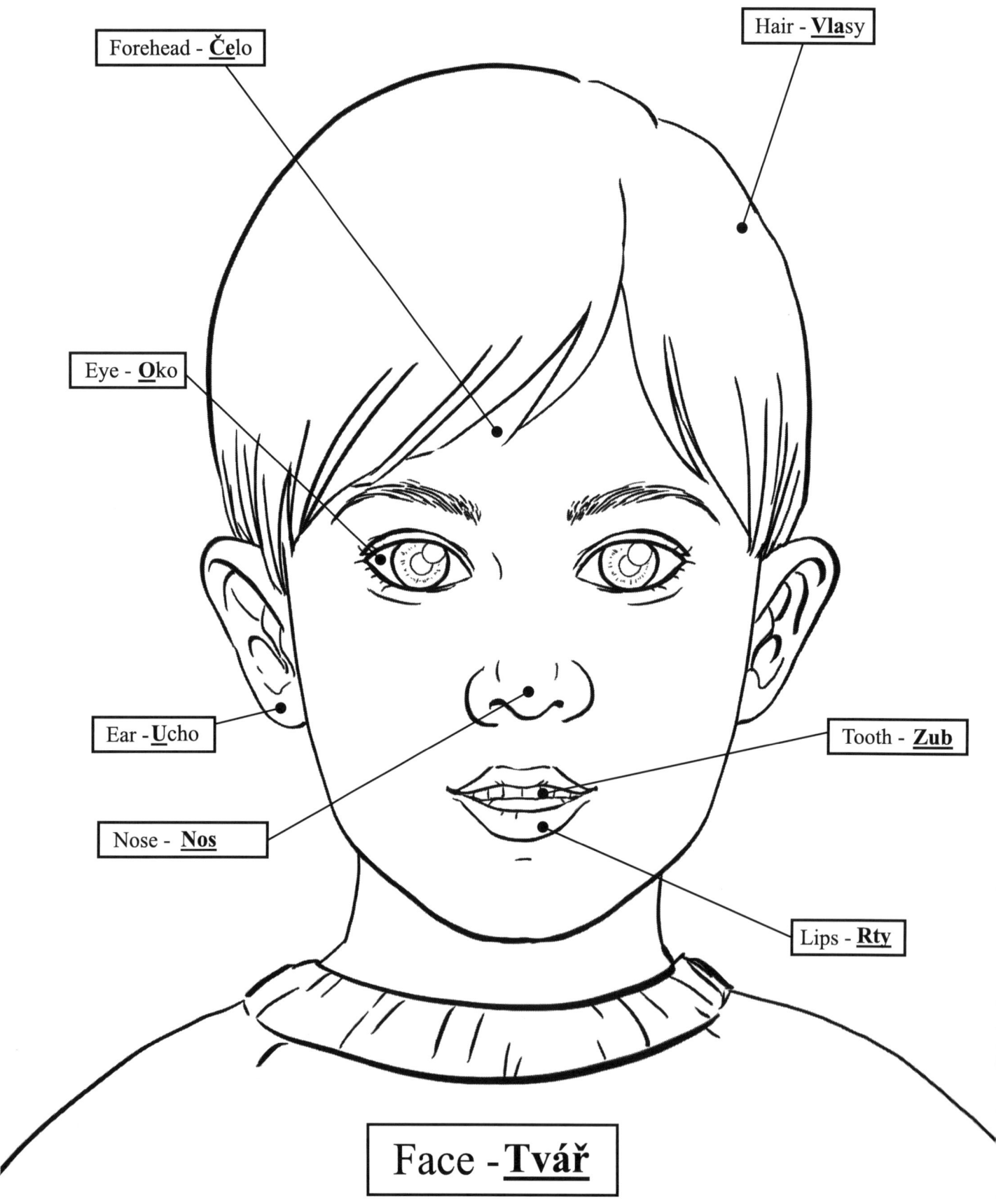

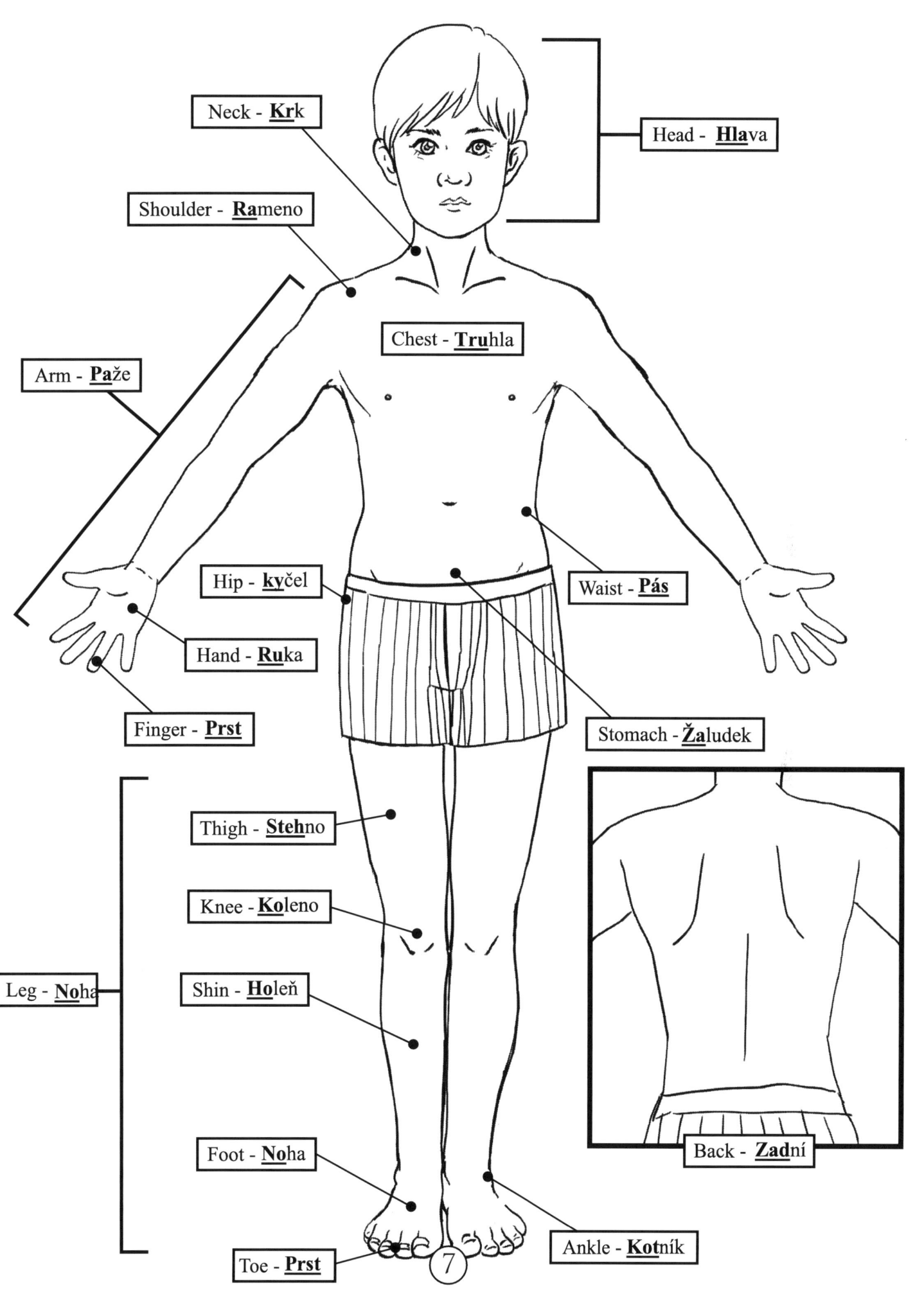

Food
Jídlo

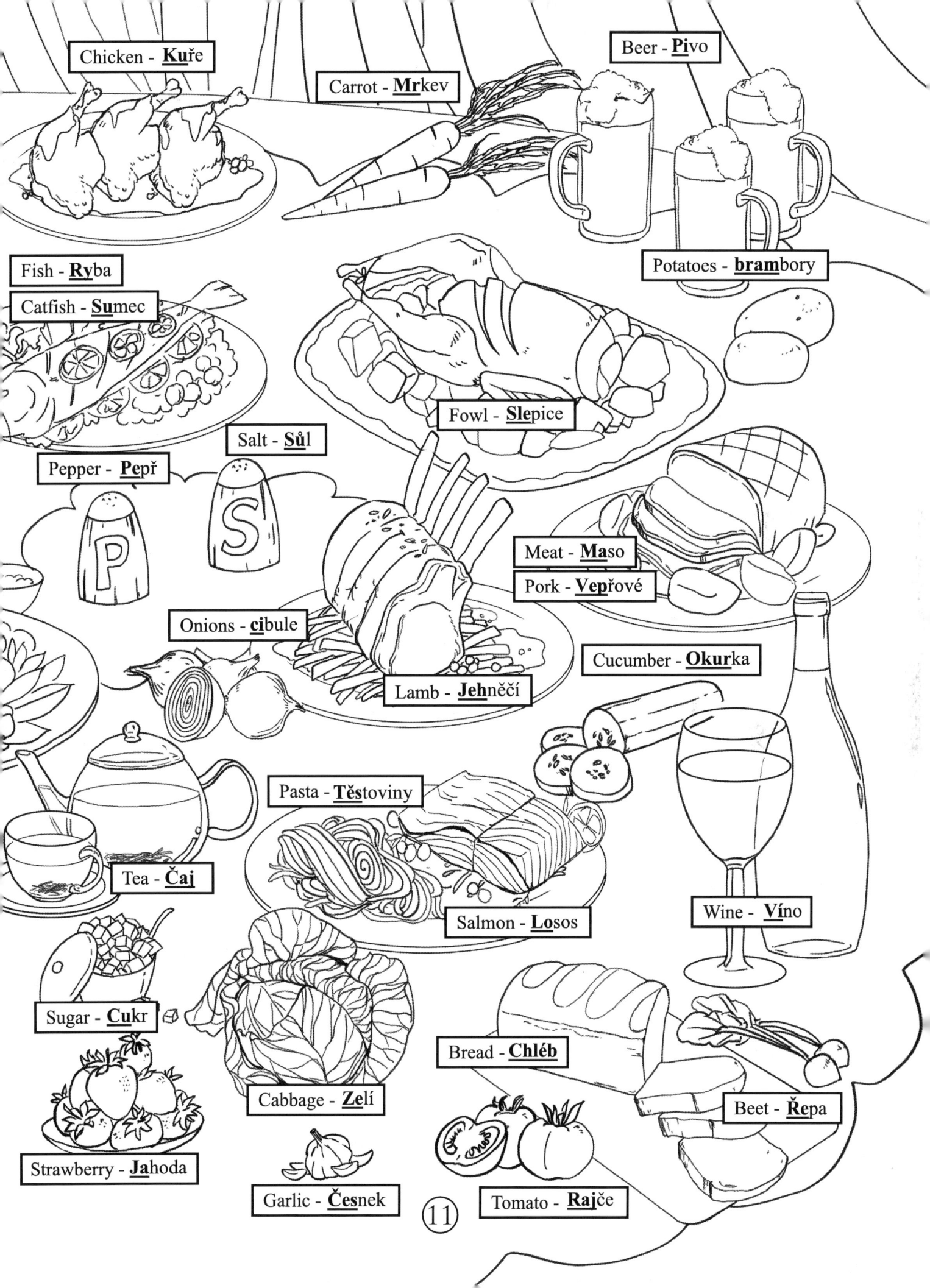

Around the house
Okolo domu

Kitchen
KUCHYNĚ

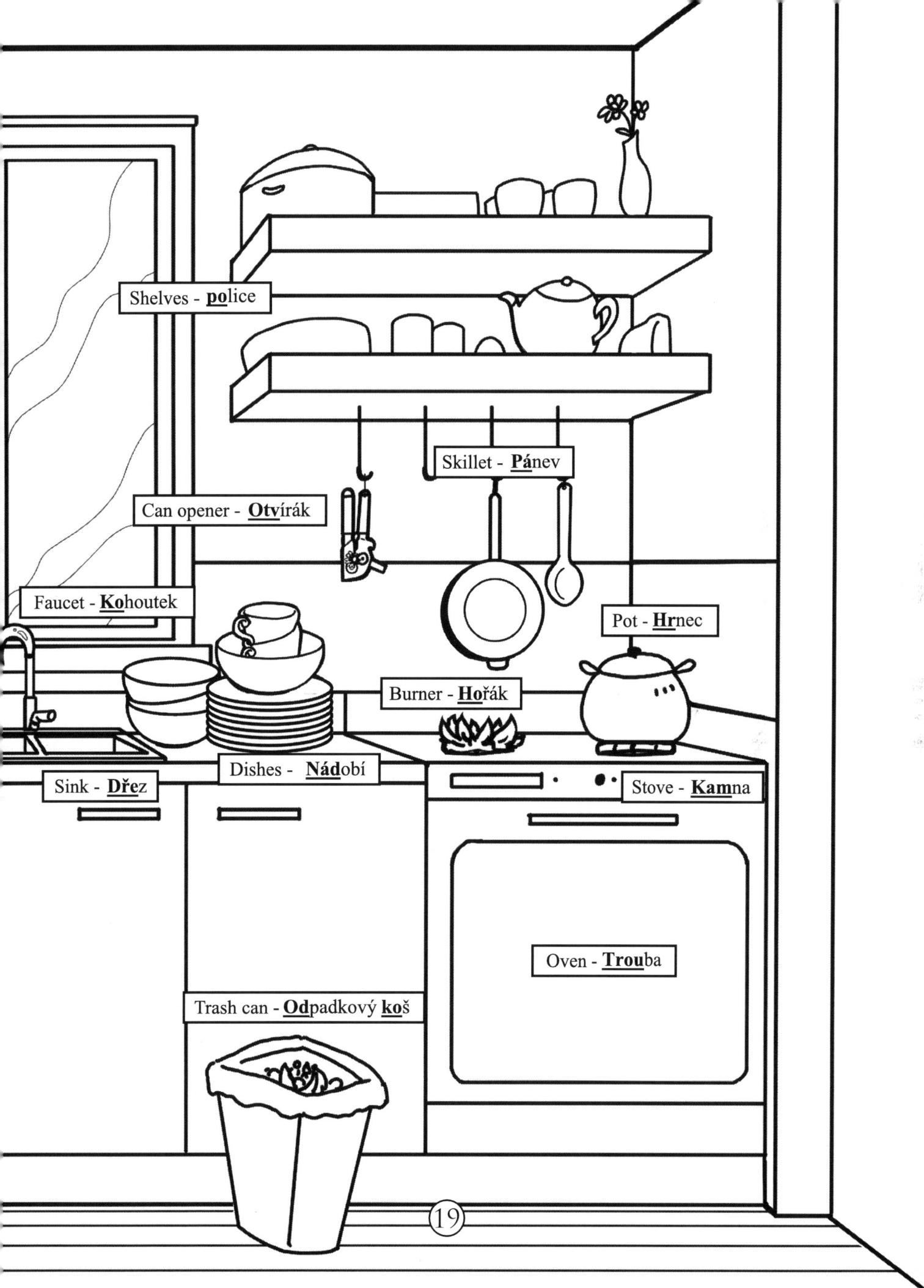

Bathroom - Dining room
KOUPELNA   JÍDELNA

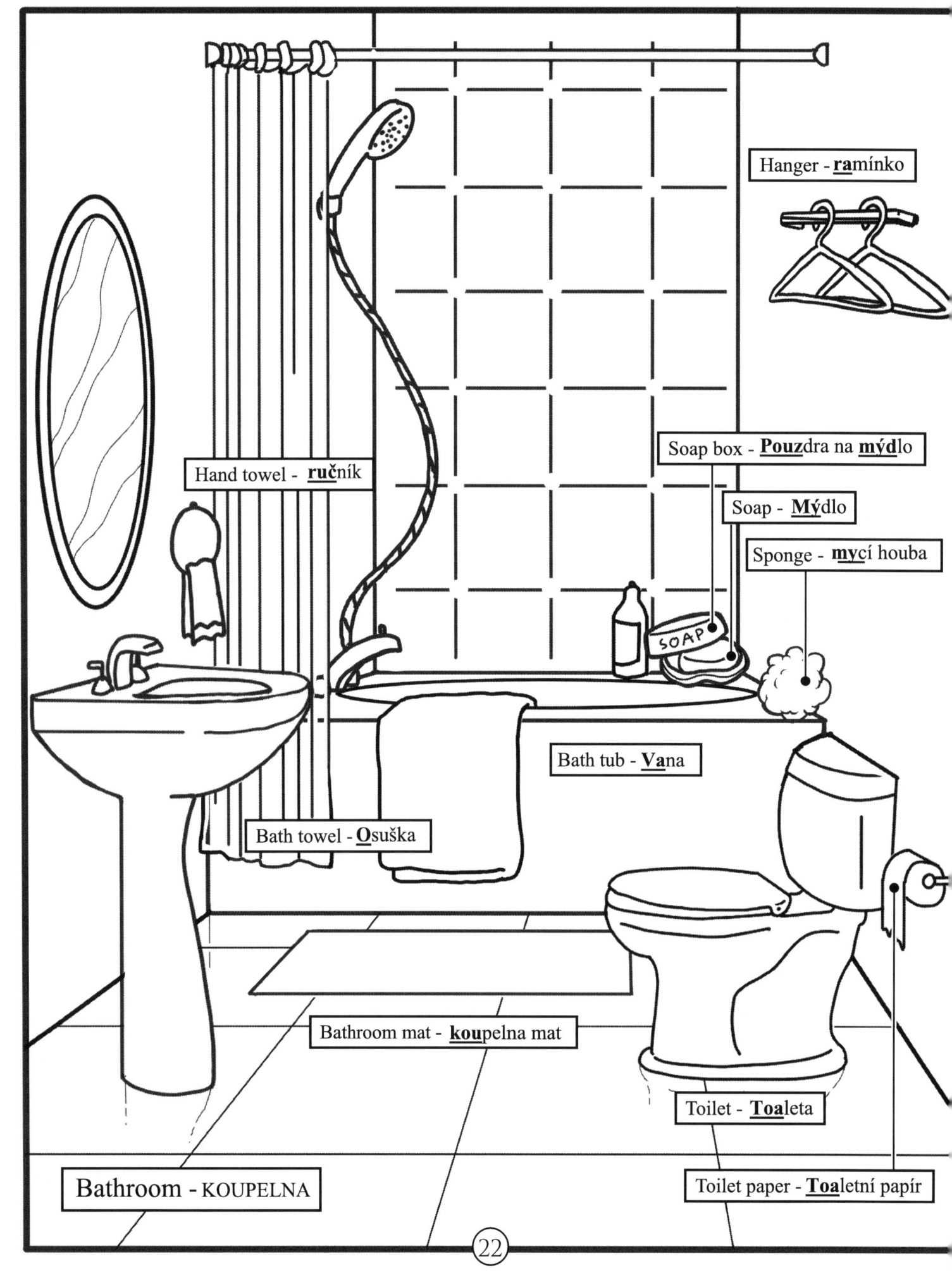

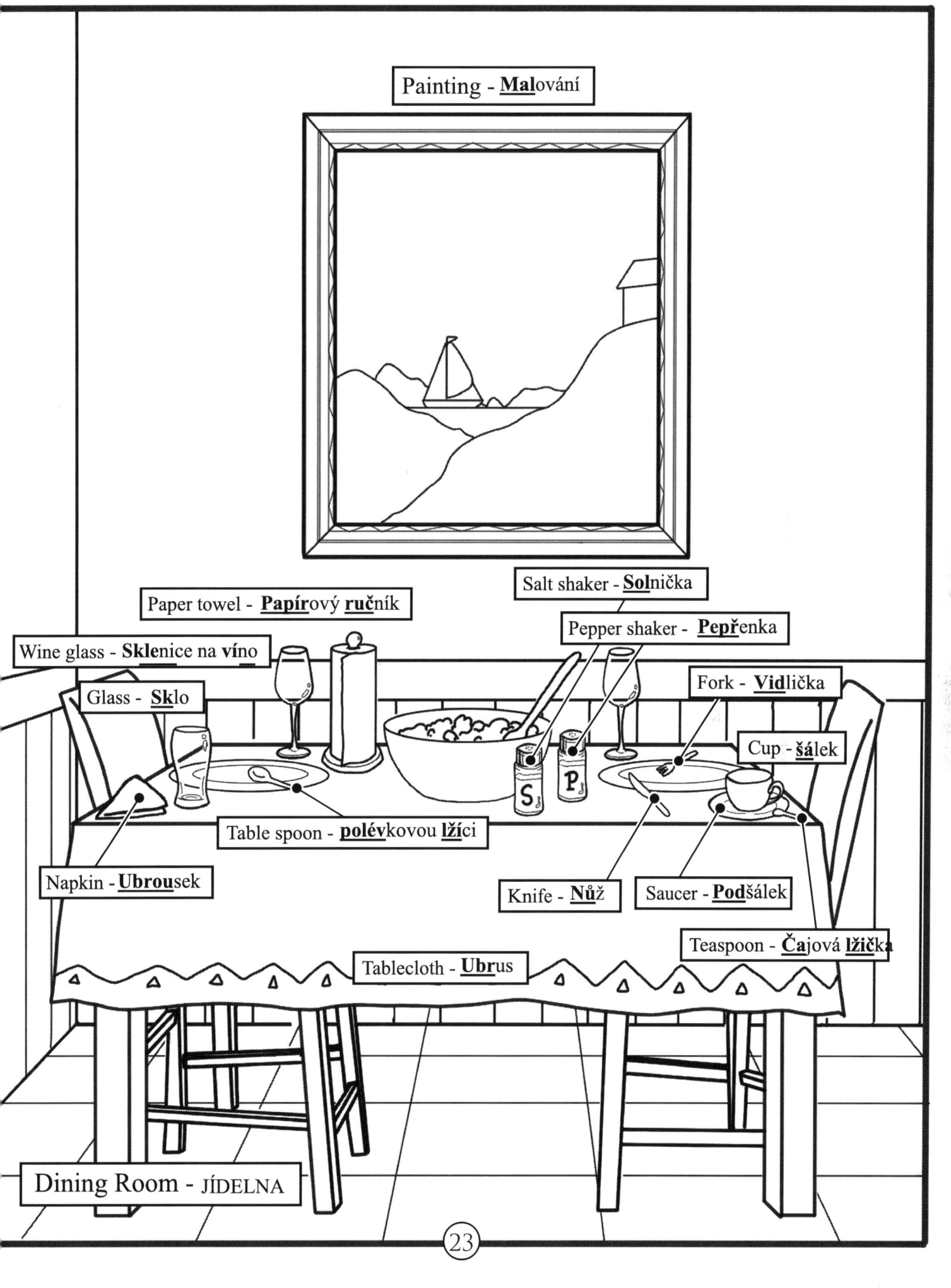

Clothes
Oblečení

Animals
Zvířata

Made in the USA
Monee, IL
23 January 2020